Bible
ESSENTIALS

Disciple Making Essentials Series

Ken Adams

Bible
ESSENTIALS

ImpactDisciples.com

BEFORE YOU BEGIN...

One of the most essential ingredients for becoming a solid disciple is having an overview of the entire Bible. Every believer needs to have a foundation of scripture in their life. They need to understand the big picture of the Bible and know how the Bible is structured.

Bible Essentials is designed to give you the overview of the Bible that you need to grow as a believer. At the end of this eight-week course, you will be able to connect the dots of scripture and understand the overall structure of the Bible. This foundational course will help guide your study of the Bible for years to come.

In order to make the most of this study, I would like to recommend a few things to guide you through the coming weeks. *First,* work through each lesson completely. The lessons will only take a few minutes to complete, so take it all in. Don't rush looking up the scriptures and writing down your answers. *Second,* commit yourself to the daily Bible readings. The scripture is designed to supplement the lesson and get you into God's Word daily. The acrostic **A.C.T.S.** will help the scripture come alive in your life. *Third,* commit yourself to the weekly memory verse. Memorizing scripture is one of the most important disciplines for spiritual growth. *Finally,* be present at the group meetings. Participation in the weekly meeting will prove to be a huge part of your growth as a disciple.

Over the next few weeks, I pray that you will discover some of the essential truths of the Bible and lay a foundation for becoming a disciple of Christ.

Being and Building Disciples,

Ken Adams

WEEK ONE:
THE BOOK OF BOOKS

Goal: To get an overview of the Bible

Welcome to *Bible Essentials.* You are about to begin a journey through the Bible that many people have never taken. Over the next several weeks, you will cover all sixty-six books of the Bible from the "big-picture" point of view. We could call this view the 30,000 foot level since you will see the Bible from a wide-angle lens. You will understand how the many different parts of the Bible connect together. You will still have questions, but I am certain the next several weeks will bring the Bible more alive in your life.

Just for fun, take a minute and test your overall Bible knowledge and then check your answers at the end of the lesson.

How many books are in the Bible? _____

What are the first five Bible books called? _____

How many Old Testament books of history are there? _____

What type of literature are Psalms and Proverbs? _____

What type of literature are Isaiah, Daniel, and Malachi _____

What are the first four books of the New Testament called? _____

_____

What do we call the books Paul wrote? _____

Hopefully, you aced the test and knew all the correct answers. If not, the next several weeks will give you a great opportunity to learn how the Bible is put together. Let's begin by looking at the overall layout of the Bible.

TWO TESTAMENTS

The Bible is divided into two parts, the Old Testament and the New Testament. The word "testament" means covenant and both the Old Testament and New Testa-

Psalm 119:11

Read the passage and write out an insight on at least one of the following:

A: Attitude to change
C: Command to obey
T: Truth to believe
S: Sin to confess

☐ **MONDAY**
Genesis 12:1-9

ment are covenants between God and His people. There are thirty-nine books in the Old Testament written by twenty-eight different writers, and twenty-seven books in the New Testament written by nine different writers. The Old Testament covers a span of over two thousand years and deals with God's covenant with the Jewish people. The New Testament covers less than one hundred years and deals with God's covenant with His Church, including both Jews and Gentiles. How does Jesus describe the relationship between the Old Testament and the New Testament according to Matthew 5:17?_____

_____

THE OLD TESTAMENT

The Old Testament is divided into three different types of literature. The Old Testament is comprised of history, poetry, and prophecy. There are seventeen books of history that provide the story of God's people from creation all the way to the rebuilding of the temple in Jerusalem beginning in 536. B.C. List the history books of the Old Testament. (If you don't know them now, you will by the end of this book.) _____

_____

_____

_____

The Old Testament also includes five books of poetry. The books of poetry reflect the way several Old Testament characters related personally to God. The books of poetry provide great wisdom and expression to a person's relationship with God. What are the five books of poetry? _____

_____

_____

The third type of literature in the Old Testament is prophetic literature. There are seventeen books of prophecy from sixteen different prophets that speak to the events of God's people in Judah, Israel, and in exile in Babylon. What are the books of prophecy? _____

_____

_____

_____

_____

❑ **THURSDAY**
Isaiah 53:1-12

In 1 Corinthians 10:11 Paul states the benefits of having the Old Testament. How can the Old Testament be of benefit to us today? _____

_____

_____

THE NEW TESTAMENT

The New Testament is also divided into three types of literature. The New Testament is comprised of history, Pauline letters, and general letters. There are five historical books in the New Testament. What are those five books?_____

_____

_____

The historical books provide the outline for all the events that occur in the New Testament. The remaining twenty-two books all fit within the timeline of the historical books.

❑ **FRIDAY**
Ezekiel 36:22-
38

The Apostle Paul wrote the second section of books in the New Testament. Paul wrote a total of thirteen books to individuals or groups of people. Many of Paul's books were written to churches he had started or to leaders he had trained. List the books Paul wrote. _____

_____

_____

The remaining nine books of the New Testament are called the General Epistles. Written by several different authors, these books were written to both individuals and groups of people. Write the books included in the General Epistles. _____

_____

_____

3

How does Hebrews 1:1-2 describe some of the differences between the Old Testament and the New Testament? _____

_____

_____

POINTS TO CONSIDER

God has revealed Himself! The Old and New Testaments are the written revelation of God. In other words, God has made Himself known to man by inspiring His words to be recorded so that man might know Him. What does 2 Timothy 3:16 say?

_____

_____

More could be written! The Bible does not contain everything we could possibly know. It does include, however, everything God wants us to know. What does John 21:25 say? _____

_____

_____

The more you get into God's Word, the more it gets into you! What does 2 Timothy 2:15 encourage you to do? _____

_____

_____

Spend time in the Bible and get to know what it says. The more you know the Bible, the more you will know about God and how He wants you to live.

Having an overview of the Bible is like having a skeleton to put muscle on. Let this quick overview be the foundation for learning more about the Bible. It is essential to be the disciple God wants you to be!

Answers to quiz: 66, Pentateuch, 17, Poetry, Prophecy, Gospels, Epistles.

QUESTIONS FOR GROUP DISCUSSION
OR PERSONAL REFLECTION

➤ Open your group time with prayer and share a highlight from your life this past week.

➤ How well did you do with the Bible quiz in this lesson?

➤ Read 1 Corinthians 10:11. What are the advantages of having the Old Testament? What challenges do you face in reading the Old Testament?

➤ What is your favorite book of the Old Testament and why?

➤ Read Hebrews 1:1-2. What does this passage tell us about the heart of God? How does the passage connect to 2 Timothy 3:16?

➤ What is your favorite book of the New Testament and why?

➤ Read Hebrews 5:14 and explain how it relates to 2 Timothy 2:15.

➤ Describe your current commitment to learning the Word of God.

➤ Share a time in your life when God's Word spoke to you and helped you navigate your life.

➤ Take some time to share prayer requests and pray for each other.

WEEK TWO:
THE BOOKS OF THE LAW

Goal: To get an overview of the Pentateuch

The Greek word referring to the first five books of the Bible is "Pentateuch" which means five scrolls. In Hebrew the first five books of the Bible are referred to as the "Torah" which is translated "law" or "instruction." Within these five books, the Bible begins the story of God and man.

The Pentateuch reveals many things. It reveals man's origin. It reveals man's fall into sin. It teaches God's plan for a people called Israel. It tells the story of the first sin, the first marriage, and the first family. It takes you into the lives of the patriarchs of the nation of Israel. It walks you through the years when the Israelites were slaves in Egypt and when they journeyed through the wilderness to the Promised Land.

Take a minute and list the first five books of the Bible from memory and then take the short test to see how much you know about the Books of the Law. You can check your answers at the end of the lesson.

Where did Adam and Eve live? _____

How many sons did Noah have? _____

What was the tower called that was built after the flood? _____

Which man did God choose to start a nation with? _____

Which son was Abraham willing to sacrifice? _____

Which son received Isaac's blessing? _____

How many sons did Jacob have? _____

Which of Jacob's sons was a leader in Egypt? _____

MEMORY VERSE

Deuteronomy
6:4,5

WEEKLY BIBLE READING

Read the passage and write out an insight on at least one of the following:

A: Attitude to change
C: Command to obey
T: Truth to believe
S: Sin to confess

☐ **MONDAY**
Genesis 3:1-13

FIVE BIG BOOKS

WEEKLY BIBLE READING

Growing in your knowledge of the Bible begins with having a quick understanding of each of the five Books of the Law.

☐ **TUESDAY**
Exodus 1:1-22

Genesis: Genesis is the book of beginnings. This book gives us the beginning of the world, the beginning of humanity, and the beginning of the nation Israel. In fifty chapters we see the creation of the world, the fall of man, a worldwide flood, a promise made, and a family protected. What did God tell Abraham in Genesis 12:1?

_____

_____

How has this promise been kept through the years? __

_____

_____

Exodus: The word Exodus means "exit" or "departure," which describes exactly what happened during Israel's exodus from Egypt. After four hundred years of slavery, the Israelites exited Egypt en route to the Promised Land. The forty chapters of Exodus describe how

☐ **WEDNESDAY**
Leviticus 26:1-13

God used Moses to lead His people out of bondage in Egypt. How does Exodus 6:6 summarize the Book of Exodus? _____

_____

_____

Leviticus: The twenty-seven chapters of the Book of Leviticus provide us with the commands and laws the Lord gave to Moses at Mount Sinai. The name Leviticus comes from the tribe of Israelites named after Levi. The purpose of this book is to call God's people to a life of holiness. How does Leviticus 20:7-8 describe this purpose?_____

_____

_____

_____

Numbers: The Book of Numbers recounts the story of God's people traveling from Egypt to the Promised Land. The name of the book comes from the two censuses Moses took during their travels in the wilderness. In thirty-six chapters the people are often found grumbling and complaining, but God's mercy remains constant. What does Numbers 14:18 say? _____

_____

_____

☐ **THURSDAY**
Numbers
13:25-33

Deuteronomy: Deuteronomy means, "Second law." The thirty-four chapters of Deuteronomy are a re-telling of the law by Moses as the people prepare to enter the Promised Land. Given as a covenant renewal, the Book of Deuteronomy reminds the second generation of Israelites that God is a faithful God who desires faithfulness in return.

What does God desire from His people according to Deuteronomy 4:29? _____

_____

_____

MAJOR EVENTS

If someone asked you to sum up all the content in the first five books of the Bible, what would you say? With so many stories and so much information, summing up the Pentateuch would be difficult, but here are a few of the major events you would certainly want to include.

☐ **FRIDAY**
Deuteronomy
6:1-19

Creation: One of the key events in the Pentateuch is obviously the creation of the world and mankind. The Bible does not tell us everything regarding creation, but it does tell us the significant things we need to know. The Bible tells us the "who," the "how," and the "why" of creation. The Bible makes it clear that God created man, out of nothing, in order to have a relationship with him. What does Genesis 1:31 tell us about creation?

_____

_____

The Fall: A second major event in the Pentateuch is the fall of man into sin. When Adam and Eve gave into Satan's temptation they created a separation between God and man that would affect every single person. What does Romans 5:19 say about Adam's sin? _____

_____

_____

The Flood: The flood recorded in Genesis 6-9 is one of the major events that took place in the Pentateuch. The flood was God's plan to destroy the sinful place the world had become and start civilization over again with a man named Noah. How is this stated in Genesis 6:7-8? _

_____

_____

_____

A Family: The next major event in the Bible took place when God chose to use Abraham and his descendants to bless the nations. God had a plan to bless a nation of people and use that nation to bless the other nations of the earth. What did God tell Abraham in Genesis 12:2? _____

_____

_____

_____

Egyptian Bondage: The chosen nation of Israel ends up living as slaves in the country of Egypt. This turn of events actually served to protect the people during a famine, but it ended with the nation of Israel being enslaved for four hundred years. What happened to Israel while they were slaves in Egypt according to Exodus 1:7? _____

_____

_____

_____

Wilderness Journey: Once Moses led the people out of bondage in Egypt, the people of Israel began a forty-year journey in the wilderness while traveling to the

Promised Land. During this journey God prepared His people for life in their new land. How is this expressed in Exodus 29:45-46? _____

_____

_____

_____

Answers to quiz: Eden, 3, Babel, Abraham, Isaac, Jacob, 12, Joseph.

QUESTIONS FOR GROUP DISCUSSION
OR PERSONAL REFLECTION

➤ Open your group time with prayer and share a highlight from your life this past week.

➤ How well did you do on the Bible quiz in this lesson?

➤ Which of the Books of the Law are you most familiar with and why? What is one of your favorite stories in the Books of the Law?

➤ Read Exodus 2:23-24. How does this passage connect to Genesis 12:2 and what does it teach you concerning God's character?

➤ How do the events that happened in Genesis 3 still affect people to this very day?

➤ Read Genesis 50:20. How has something meant for harm in your life turned out to be for good?

➤ Read Exodus 16:12. What does this verse teach us about the wilderness times in life? How has God been with you during times in the wilderness?

➤ Which patriarch — Abraham, Isaac, Jacob, or Joseph — can you most relate to and why?

➤ Take some time to share prayer requests and pray for each other.

WEEK THREE:
THE BOOKS OF HISTORY

Goal: To gain an overview of Israel's history

Everyone has heard the phrase "history repeats it-self." We see that to be true in the Bible as well. Much of what we see taking place in the world today has already happened in the journey of the nation of Israel.

Israel's journey from entering into the Promised Land to being freed from exile in Babylon is recorded in a section of the Bible commonly called the Books of History. These twelve books recount the history of the Nation of Israel from around 1400 B.C. to about 425 B.C. These twelve books tell the story of how Abraham's descendants conquered the land of promise, how they lived in the land and returned to the land after being tak-en captive in Babylon. You can learn a great deal about God and how to relate to Him by reading the Books of History.

Take a minute to list the Books of History and take the short test to see how much you know about these books. You can check your answers at the end of the lesson. __

_____

_____

Who led Israel after Moses died? _____

What was the first city conquered in the Promised Land? _____

Which judge had great strength? _____

Who was the first king of Israel? _____

What was the Southern Kingdom called? _____

Which Moabite woman is a Book of History written about? _____

Which king was known for having wisdom? _____

Who led the rebuilding of Israel's wall? _____

MEMORY VERSE

Joshua 1:8

WEEKLY BIBLE READING

Read the passage and write out an insight on at least one of the following:

A: Attitude to change
C: Command to obey
T: Truth to believe
S: Sin to confess

☐ **MONDAY**
Joshua 1:1-18

HISTORY MAJORS

One of the best and easiest ways to learn more about the Books of History is to identify the three major categories into which all twelve of the History books can fall. All twelve History Books can be divided into three sections of history.

Books of Conquest: The Books of Conquest are comprised of the books of Joshua, Judges, and Ruth. These books recount the history of when the Israelites entered and settled the Promised Land. How does Joshua 21:43 summarize the Books of Conquest?

_____

_____

What does this period of history teach us today according to Joshua 21:45?_____

_____

_____

Books of Kings: The Books of Kings include the books of 1 & 2 Samuel, 1 & 2 Kings, and 1 & 2 Chronicles. These books provide the history of how Israel was governed under the leadership of a number of different kings while the nation was first united and then later divided. One observation that can be made from every king of Israel is that they either did what was right or they did evil in the eyes of God. In other words, each king of Israel was either a godly leader or a self-centered leader. How does 1 Samuel 16:7 describe the key to godly leadership? _____

_____

_____

How do you see this principle still being played out today?

_____

_____

Books of Exile and Return: The Books of Exile and Return include Ezra, Nehemiah, and Esther. These books give the history of how the nation of Israel went into exile in Babylon and then returned to restore Israel. How was the destruction of Jerusalem described in 2 Chronicles 36:17-20? _____

_____

How was the return to Jerusalem described in Ezra 2:1? _____

_____

_____

How does the story of captivity and restoration continue to happen in individual lives to this day? _____

_____

_____

THE "TOP TEN" OF HISTORY

One way to learn more about the Books of History is to study some of the key figures in this period of time. These twelve books are filled with stories of how God worked in the lives of different people. There are ten people, however, that provide a good snapshot of the Books of History.

Joshua: Joshua gives leadership to the nation of Israel after the death of Moses. He leads the people into the Promised Land and provides strategic spiritual leadership for the Jewish people at this time in history. How does Joshua demonstrate key leadership according to Joshua 24:15? _____

_____

_____

Gideon: Gideon served as one of the twelve Judges for Israel. His story is recorded in Judges, chapters 6-8. God used Gideon to destroy the Midianites and bring peace to the people of Israel. What did Israel want Gideon to do according to Judges 8:22?

_____

_____

☐ **THURSDAY**
1 Kings 3:1-15

☐ **FRIDAY**
1 Chronicles
29:1-13

Samson: Samson is one of the most famous characters in the Bible. He is known primarily for his great strength. God used Samson's strength while he was leading Israel as a judge. What condition was Israel in during Samson's days according to Judges 14:4?_____

_____
_____
_____

What was Samson's downfall as a leader according to Judges 16:1? _____

_____
_____
_____

Ruth: The Book that bears Ruth's name is one of the greatest love stories of all time. Ruth was a young Moabite woman who left her own people to be with her Jewish mother-in-law Naomi. The story of Ruth is a great reminder of love and faithfulness. What famous verse comes from Ruth 1:16? _____

_____
_____

Samuel: Samuel served the people of Israel as a prophet and Judge. Samuel led the people during the transition from being led by rulers to being led by a king. What was said of Samuel in 1 Samuel 3:19? _____

_____
_____
_____

Saul: Saul was chosen to be the first king over Israel. Going against God's will, the Israelites demanded a king, and Saul became a prideful leader. What did God say about Saul in 1 Samuel 15:11? _____

_____
_____
_____

What does 1 Samuel 15:35 say about the Lord?_____

_____

_____

David: David became the king of Israel following Saul. And David was God's choice. How was David described in 1 Samuel 13:14? _____

_____

_____

God used David to lead Israel to peace and prosperity, and through his lineage would one day come the Messiah! What does Romans 1:3 say? _____

_____

_____

_____

Solomon: Solomon was David's son and followed David as King of Israel. What did Solomon ask God for according to
1 Kings 3:9? _____

_____

_____

_____

How did God answer Solomon according to 1 Kings 3:12?

_____

_____

Esther: Esther was a Jewish woman who became queen of Persia while Israel was exiled in Babylon. What did her uncle say to her in Esther 4:14? _____

_____

_____

Esther played a significant role in the survival of the Jewish people while they were captive in Babylon.

Nehemiah: The Book of Nehemiah is named after the man who led the people of Israel to rebuild the wall around Jerusalem. Nehemiah demonstrated great leadership in helping the people rebuild the wall in record time. How long did it take to rebuild the wall according to Nehemiah 6:15? _____

_____

_____

Answers to quiz: Joshua, Jericho, Samson, Saul, Judah, Ruth, Solomon, Nehemiah

QUESTIONS FOR GROUP DISCUSSION
OR PERSONAL REFLECTION

➤ Open your group time with prayer and share a praise from your week.

➤ Which of the "Top Ten" characters do you most identify with, and why?

➤ Read Joshua 1:13. How does the Promised Land relate to your life today? What is keeping you from entering your Promised Land?

➤ Read Judges 21:25. How does the condition of Israel compare to our world today? How can our condition be changed?

➤ Read 1 Samuel 16:7. Why did God choose David? How should we see leadership today? Why is there a leadership crisis in our world today?

➤ Read Ezra 7:10. How did Ezra's actions impact the restoration of Israel? How could this example change our world today?

➤ Take some time to share prayer requests and pray for each other.

WEEK FOUR:
THE BOOKS OF WISDOM

MEMORY VERSE

Goal: To gain an overview of the Wisdom Books

If you could sit down with the wisest person you knew for a few minutes every morning, would you do it? I'm sure you would and that would be a very good investment of your time. Another good investment of your time would be to take a few minutes each day and read from the Wisdom Books of the Bible. A few minutes in Psalms or Proverbs each day could have a profound impact on the direction of your life.

The Books of Wisdom, or often called the Books of Poetry, are some of the most inspirational writings in the Bible. This section of biblical literature is comprised of five books. What are the Books of Wisdom? _____

_____

_____

_____

These books filled with wisdom for living are written by some of the wisest people that ever lived. Let's start our study of these books with a short quiz and see how wise you are. You can check your answers at the end of the lesson.

Proverbs 4:23

WEEKLY BIBLE READING

Read the passage and write out an insight on at least one of the following:

A: Attitude to change
C: Command to obey
T: Truth to believe
S: Sin to confess

☐ **MONDAY**
Job 1:1-22

Job is known for his? _____

Most of the Psalms were written by? _____

Most of the Proverbs were written by? _____

Ecclesiastes was written by? _____

Song of Songs was written by? _____

WORDS OF WISDOM

WEEKLY BIBLE READING

☐ **TUESDAY**
Psalm 1:1-6

In order to really know your Bible, you need to be familiar with the main objective of each Book of Wisdom. Here is a quick overview to each of these five books.

Job - The Book of Suffering: Job is the perfect example of bad things happening to good people. How is Job described in Job 1:1? _____

_____

_____

Job consists of many different conversations. The first is between God and Satan regarding Job. What did God tell Satan in Job 1:12? _____

_____

_____

Most of the book is comprised of Job's conversations with a handful of friends. Who were a few of those friends according to Job 2:11? _____

_____

_____

☐ **WEDNESDAY**
Proverbs 3:1-12

Another key conversation in the Book of Job is between God and Job. What does Job tell God in Job 42:2? _____

_____

_____

Truth: Job's words remind us that God is a sovereign Lord!

Psalm - The Book of Praise: The Book of Psalms is a hymnbook. It is a collection of songs that were sung by the Hebrew people during times of worship. David wrote the majority of the psalms, which are typically divided into five sections or arrangements. The Book of Psalms contains the longest chapter in the Bible (Psalm 119) and the shortest chapter in the Bible (Psalm 117). The psalms cover the full range of human emotion and experience. Write down Psalm 150:6 _____

_____

_____

Truth: The Lord desires and deserves your praise!

Proverbs - The Book of Wisdom: Solomon wrote most of the nearly one thousand Proverbs. They are packed full of godly and practical wisdom for living. Proverbs provides nuggets of wisdom for a wide range of subjects, including money, relationships, communication, work, and parenting. You will never completely mine all the gold contained in this book. What does Proverbs 1:7 say about wisdom? _____

☐ **THURSDAY**
Ecclesiastes
3:1-15

_____

_____

Truth: You would be wise to read one of the thirty-one proverbs every day!

Ecclesiastes - The Book of Meaning and Purpose: Solomon is believed to be the writer of the Book of Ecclesiastes. Ecclesiastes means "preacher" and in it Solomon preaches on the meaning and purpose to life. In concluding his search to find meaning and purpose in life, what did the preacher say in Ecclesiastes 12:13? _____

☐ **FRIDAY**
Song of Songs
8:1-14

_____

_____

Truth: Life in one statement — Fear God and keep His commandments!

Song of Songs - The Book of Love: Song of Songs is a love story of Solomon and his bride. It is also a beautiful picture of Christ's love for His church. This book is written as a dialogue between a husband and his wife. What does the husband say to his wife in chapter four verse one?_____

_____

_____

**PRAYER
REQUESTS**

KNOW YOUR POETS

The Book of Job: The authorship of Job is unknown, but the main character is clear. The story of Job is a story about a righteous man who loses everything and chooses to trust God regardless. Many scholars believe the Book of Job was written by Moses and actually took place during the time of Abraham, Isaac, and Jacob. Regardless of when and who wrote the Book of Job, all people in every generation can relate to the problem of suffering. How does Job 1:21 serve as a great reminder of how to deal with loss and suffering?_____
_____
_____

The Book of Psalms: The Psalms were written over a period of thousands of years, so you can conclude that there were a number of different authors. David wrote seventy-five psalms. A priest named Asaph wrote twelve psalms. The sons of Korah wrote ten psalms. Solomon wrote two psalms, and Moses wrote one psalm. Fifty of the psalms have no identified author. Who wrote Psalm 101:1? _____

How does that Psalm serve as a theme for all the psalms? _____
_____
_____

The Book of Proverbs: Solomon wrote many more proverbs than the one's recorded in the Book of Proverbs. How many proverbs and songs did Solomon write according to 1 Kings 4:32? _____
_____
_____

Who helped compile the proverbs of Solomon according to Proverbs 25:1?_____

Who wrote Proverbs 30 and 31 according to the first verses in those chapters?_____

The Book of Ecclesiastes: Most Bible scholars believe that Solomon wrote the Book of Ecclesiastes. The most convincing piece of evidence is found in the first verse of the book. How does the author identify himself? _____

How does the author describe himself in Ecclesiastes 12:9?

_____

_____

The Book of Song of Songs: Who is identified as the author of this book according to the first verse of the first chapter? _____

_____

The book includes three main characters. Solomon is known as the "beloved." Solomon's Shulamite wife is referred to as the "lover." The third main character is actually a group of people called the "friends or others," who were attendants to the bride.

What does the bride profess in Songs of Songs 6:3?_

_____

_____

Who refers to the Books of Wisdom in Luke 24:44?

_____

If Jesus knew the Books of Wisdom, it might be worth your time to know them as well!

Answers to quiz: patience, David, Solomon, Solomon, Solomon.

QUESTIONS FOR GROUP DISCUSSION
OR PERSONAL REFLECTION

➤ Open your group with a prayer and share a highlight from your week.

➤ Which of the Wisdom Books is your favorite and why?

➤ Read Job 1:20-22. How did Job deal with loss in his life? How should we respond to trials and difficulties in our lives today?

➤ Read Psalm 150. What lessons do we learn from this short chapter? How is the priority of praise expressed in your own life?

➤ Read Proverbs 1:1-3. How would you describe the difference between wisdom and knowledge? Read Proverbs 1:7. What should be our attitude towards wisdom?

➤ Read Ecclesiastes 4:9-12. What are the benefits of partnership according to this passage? Explain the three-fold cord in verse 12.

➤ Read Song of Songs 1:15-16. How does a married couple keep the flame of love burning in a marriage? How does our relationship with God relate to the husband and wife relationship?

➤ Take some time to share prayer requests and pray for each other.

WEEK FIVE: THE BOOKS OF PROPHECY

Goal: To gain an overview of the Prophetic Books

Some of the most interesting characters in the Bible are the Old Testament prophets. A large fish swallowed one prophet. One prophet married a prostitute. One Old Testament prophet lay on his side for over three hundred days. Needless to say, the Books of Prophecy are quite colorful and a very interesting read. Everyone should take time to know and understand the Books of Prophecy.

The English word "prophet" originates from two Greek words. The first word "pro" means *in place of*, and the second word "phemi" means *to speak*. Thus the word "prophet" means *one who speaks in place of another*.

Prophets were men who spoke to the people on behalf of God. There are seventeen Books of Prophecy and they comprise one-fourth of the entire Bible. These seventeen books are typically broken into two categories called the Major and Minor Prophets. The only difference between the two categories is the size of the books. The five Major Prophets are larger than the twelve Minor Prophets.

Take a minute to list all seventeen Books of Prophecy and then take the short quiz to see how much you already know about the Prophets. You can check your answers at the end of the lesson. Name the Books of Prophecy. _____

_____

_____

_____

_____

_____

_____

MEMORY VERSE

Habakkuk 3:19

WEEKLY BIBLE READING

Read the passage and write out an insight on at least one of the following:

A: Attitude to change
C: Command to obey
T: Truth to believe
S: Sin to confess

☐ **MONDAY**
Isaiah 9:1-7

Who is the "weeping" prophet? _____

Which prophet was in a lions' den? _____

Which prophet lay on his side for 390 days? _____

Which prophet married a prostitute? _____

Which prophet warns of locusts? _____

Which prophet had eight visions? _____

WHO, WHEN, WHERE?

One of the best ways to understand the Books of Prophecy is to see where and when they fit in the Bible and in history. You can divide all the Books of Prophecy into three different periods of time. Some prophets spoke before Israel was taken into exile in Babylon. Some prophets spoke while the people of Israel were in exile, and others spoke after they were released from exile. These three time periods make it very easy to understand which prophet was speaking at what time and why he was speaking. Here is a quick overview of each time frame.

Prophets *before* **the exile:** Eleven Prophets spoke before Israel was taken into exile in Babylon. Obadiah spoke to the nation of Edom. Jonah and Nahum spoke to the Assyrians in Nineveh. Isaiah, Jeremiah, Micah, Zephaniah, and Joel spoke to the southern kingdom of Judah. Hosea and Amos spoke to the northern kingdom of Israel. Habakkuk spoke to all the people of God.

The central theme in all of these prophecies is God's warning and the need to repent. God can only allow disobedience and sin to continue for so long. At some point God must judge sin and bring about justice. How does 2 Kings 20:16-17 demonstrate God's warning and judgment? _____

_____

_____

_____

Prophets *during* **the exile:** There were two prophets that spoke for God while the people of Israel were captives in Babylon. These two prophets were Ezekiel and Daniel.

A central theme from the prophets Ezekiel and Daniel would be a message to remain faithful in times of difficulty. As the Israelites lived as captives in a foreign land, the Lord used Ezekiel and Daniel to speak to them and encourage them to stay committed to Him and not get caught up in Babylonian culture. What happened to God's people according to 2 Chronicles 36:17-21? _____

☐ **THURSDAY**
Daniel 1:1-21

_____

_____

_____

Prophets *after* **the exile:** The Lord spoke through three prophets after the Israelites had been released from Babylon. These Prophets included Haggai, Zechariah, and Malachi.

After seventy years of captivity, the Persian King Cyrus released the Israelites and allowed them to return home and rebuild the city of Jerusalem. During this time the Jewish people were lead by Zerubbabel, Nehemiah, and Ezra. The central theme of the prophets during this time was "restoration." God wanted his people to experience spiritual, national, and physical restoration. What did God tell his people through Zechariah in Zechariah 8:7-8? _____

☐ **FRIDAY**
Jonah 2:1-10

_____

_____

_____

THE PROPHETS' JOB DESCRIPTION

PRAYER REQUESTS

_____

_____

_____

_____

_____

_____

_____

_____

_____

_____

_____

_____

_____

_____

_____

_____

_____

_____

As we have already seen, the role of a prophet is to speak to the people on behalf of God. At times this meant _forthtelling_ and at other times it meant _foretelling_. The prophets declared God's truth to His people, and they also told of future events yet to come. In declaring these two messages, the prophets fulfilled the following tasks for God.

They exposed sin! God used the prophets to speak to the people concerning their sin and disobedience to Him. Proclaiming this type of message was not always popular with the people. Many times being a prophet of God meant being seen as an enemy of the people. How does Isaiah 1:2 illustrate this point? _____

_____

_____

_____

They called people to repentance! God used the prophets to call His people back into a right relationship with Himself. God was always seeking to restore His relationship with His people, and the prophets urged the people to repent. How does Ezekiel 3:21 describe this role of the prophet? _____

_____

_____

_____

They warned against coming judgment! At times the Lord would bring judgment against His people when they refused to repent. The prophets were instrumental in warning God's people about these times of judgment. How does Amos 7:17 demonstrate the role of warning by a prophet? _____

_____

_____

_____

They predicted the Messiah's coming! God used the prophets to tell the people about the coming of the Messiah. It is hard to see how so many people missed Jesus when His coming was so clearly predicted. What did Isaiah say about the Messiah in Isaiah 7:14?_____

_____

_____

_____

One more important observation about prophets is that God did not take a "false prophet" lightly. How was a false prophet handled in Jeremiah 28:15-17? _____

_____

_____

_____

Answers to quiz: Jeremiah, Daniel, Ezekiel, Hosea, Joel, Zechariah

QUESTIONS FOR GROUP DISCUSSION
OR PERSONAL REFLECTION

➤ Open your group with prayer and share an insight God has been teaching you.

➤ How much time have you spent reading the Books of Prophecy compared to other books in the Bible? Why do you think this is?

➤ Do you have a favorite Book of Prophecy or a favorite passage from a prophet?

➤ Take a few minutes to discuss the three time frames in which the prophets spoke. What would have been different about each prophecy?

➤ Read Isaiah 61:1-2. What connection does this passage have with Jesus? Read Luke 4:14-20. How did people respond to what Jesus read?

➤ Read Jeremiah 29:11. How did this verse relate to God's people years ago? How can it relate today?

➤ Read Daniel 1:8-16. How does this story speak to our lives today? In what ways are you feeling pressured by our culture?

➤ Read Joel 2:28-29 and Acts 2:16-21. How are these passages connected? What does this connection say to you about prophecy?

➤ Read Jonah 2:1 and 4:2. Have you ever had a Jonah experience in your life?

➤ Take some time to share prayer requests and pray for each othe

WEEK SIX: THE BOOKS OF THE GOSPELS AND ACTS

Goal: To get an overview of the New Testament history

The history of the New Testament is discovered in the Gospels of Jesus and the Acts of the Apostles. These five books provide an account of the life and work of Jesus and His Apostles. For most people these five books are some of the most popular books in the entire Bible. They provide a front row look at what Jesus did and said as well as the work the Holy Spirit did through the lives of the Apostles. In some ways all five of these books could actually be called the "Acts of Jesus and His Apostles."

There were four hundred years between the Old Testament and the New Testament in which God was completely silent. God broke that silence with the cry of a baby — a baby named Jesus. In the life of Jesus, God spoke and He began a new covenant with mankind. Through the Apostles this covenant was spread to all nations.

List the four Gospel Books and then take the short quiz to see how much you know about the Gospels and Acts. _____

_____

_____

What was Matthew's original occupation? _____

Where was Jesus born? _____

Who baptized Jesus? _____

What was Luke's occupation? _____

Where was the church first planted? _____

MEMORY VERSE

Luke 9:23

WEEKLY BIBLE READING

Read the passage and write out an insight on at least one of the following:

A: Attitude to change
C: Command to obey
T: Truth to believe
S: Sin to confess

☐ **MONDAY**
Matthew 3:1-17

A FOUR-ACT STORY

WEEKLY BIBLE READING

☐ **TUESDAY**
Mark 16:1-20

Act One: From Heaven to Earth! Jesus was here on a mission. He left the majesty and splendor of heaven to accomplish an assignment here on earth. Jesus couldn't have stated His mission any clearer than He did in Luke 19:10. Why did Jesus leave heaven and come to earth? __

_____

_____

Our mission in life is the same as Christ's. How are you doing at seeking the lost and leading them to Jesus?_

_____

_____

Act Two: From Bethlehem to Calvary! Jesus lived on earth and became a model for all to follow. Jesus made it very clear that He was the model He wanted everyone to follow. What did Jesus say in John 14:12?___

_____

_____

☐ **WEDNESDAY**
Luke 5:1-16

If we claim to be Christians, we are to live the life Jesus lived by His power at work within us. What does 1 John 2:6 teach?

_____

_____

Are you walking like Jesus walked these days? _____

Act Three: From the Grave to Glory! One of the things that separated Jesus from everyone else on the planet is His resurrection from the dead. What was said about Jesus in Matthew 28:6? _____

_____

_____

The resurrected Lord appeared to His disciples several times before He departed for heaven. Where did they see Jesus according to Matthew 28:16? _____

_____

The resurrection of Jesus changed everything for the disciples and it changes everything for us as well. Why is the resurrection so important? _____

_____

_____

Act Four: From Jerusalem to the Ends of the Earth! Before Jesus made His return to heaven, He gave His disciples their marching orders until He returned. What did Jesus tell His disciples to do according to Matthew 28:19-20? _____

_____

_____

What did Jesus say in Acts 1:8? _____

_____

_____

The commission Jesus gave to "make disciples of all nations" has not been fulfilled. That challenge to take the message to the ends of the earth is still our challenge today. How committed are you to helping fulfill the commission to "make disciples of all nations"?

_____

_____

☐ **THURSDAY**
John 1:1-18

☐ **FRIDAY**
Acts 1:1-26

The Gospels and Acts do read as if they were a four-part play. Beginning with Christ's birth until today, the plan of God is still in motion. The mission is still to seek and save that which is lost. The pattern which we must follow is still Jesus! The world would be a very different place if more people were fleshing out the character and conduct of Christ. Jesus is still alive and His resurrection gives us a new purpose and perspective on this life. Making disciples in your Jerusalem and beyond is still the target you should be aiming for. The story is still being written and you have a role to play in His story!

DIFFERENT VIEW POINTS

PRAYER REQUESTS

Sometimes people wonder why we have four different Gospel accounts? The answer is quite simple. We have four different accounts because we have four different audiences. Each book is about the same person but written from a different perspective. The Gospel accounts are like having four people standing on four different street corners witnessing an accident and all writing from a different vantage point. Let's look at the different viewpoints of each book.

Matthew: Matthew writes form the viewpoint of Jesus as "Messianic King." What is Jesus called in Matthew 2:2? _____

_____

The Book of Matthew is written to a Jewish audience and is filled with Old Testament references. Matthew clearly communicates that Jesus is the "Lion of the Tribe of Judah."

Mark: Mark writes from the viewpoint of Jesus as "Jehovah's Servant." How is Jesus described in Mark 10:45? _____

_____

The Book of Mark was written to a Roman audience and presents Jesus as a humble servant. Most of Mark's Gospel deals with the final days of Christ's life.

Luke: Luke writes from the viewpoint of Jesus as the "Son of Man." Luke was a physician, and gives very precise details about Jesus' life. How does Jesus refer to Himself in Luke 9:58? _____

_____

The Book of Luke is written to a Greek audience and vividly depicts the character of Christ. Luke wrote more pages of the New Testament than any other author.

John: John writes from the viewpoint of Jesus being the "Son of God." Who did Jesus claim to be in John 19:7? _____

_____

The Book of John was written to a wide range of people. John's audience was literally the entire world. The purpose for John's Gospel is very clear. What does John 20:31 say about the purpose for this book? _____

_____

_____

Acts: Luke also wrote the Book of Acts. He wrote it from the viewpoint of the "Risen Lord." What is said concerning Jesus in Acts 1:3? _____

_____

_____

The Book of Acts was written to several audiences. First, it was written to a man named Theophilus. Second, it was written for Jewish believers. Third, it was written for Gentiles. It was a record of the birth and expansion of the Church of Jesus Christ.

Answers to quiz: Tax collector, Bethlehem, John, Physician, Jerusalem

QUESTIONS FOR GROUP DISCUSSION
OR PERSONAL REFLECTION

➤ Open your group with prayer and have everyone share a story of someone you have been sharing Christ with or encouraging.

➤ As you think about the Gospels, what is one of your favorite stories or teachings?

➤ How would you explain the life of Christ to someone who had never heard of Him?

➤ Read Hebrews 1:1-4. What does this passage tell us about God? What can we learn about Jesus from this passage?

➤ Read Luke 4:18-19. In what ways did Jesus fulfill this prophecy of Isaiah? How is it still being fulfilled?

➤ Read John 3:16. How does this verse sum up the entire four Gospels and the Book of Acts?

➤ Read John 21:25. What does this verse tell us about the life of Christ?

➤ Read Acts 2:42-47. What do you think the first church was like?

➤ If Acts 29 was a chapter about how the Gospel was being spread through you, what would it say?

➤ Take some time to share prayer requests and pray for each other.

WEEK SEVEN: THE BOOKS TO CHURCHES AND PASTORS

Goal: To gain an overview of Paul's letters to churches and pastors

With the exception of Jesus, the Apostle Paul could be the greatest church planter to ever live. Over three missionary journeys, Paul started a number of churches, developed pastors for those churches, and influenced thousands of people through those churches.

The Book of Acts provides us with the record of Paul's three missionary journeys, and his letters provide us with his instruction and follow-up with the churches he planted and the pastors he trained. In thirteen letters Paul writes a very large portion of the New Testament. Nine of these books were written to churches, and four of these books were written to individuals.

Take a minute and write the names of the churches and individuals that Paul wrote letters to and then take the short quiz to see how much you know about these books. _____

_____

_____

Where did Paul's missionary journeys begin? _____

Where was Paul when he wrote Ephesians? _____

Which Apostle does Paul confront in Galatians? _____

Who was an associate of Timothy in Philippians? _____

Where did Paul send Titus? _____

Who did Paul speak to Philemon about? _____

MEMORY VERSE

Galatians 6:9

WEEKLY BIBLE READING

Read the passage and write out an insight on at least one of the following:

A: Attitude to change
C: Command to obey
T: Truth to believe
S: Sin to confess

☐ **MONDAY**
Romans 5:1-21

PLACES AND PEOPLE

WEEKLY BIBLE READING

☐ **TUESDAY**
1 Corinthians
3:1-23

☐ **WEDNESDAY**
Galatians 5:1-
26

Learning more about the letters (or epistles) of Paul begins with understanding more about the places and the people he wrote to. Here is a quick survey of the epistles of Paul.

Romans: Romans is the letter Paul wrote to the church located in the city of Rome. Rome was the capital of the world at this point in history. Who is this letter addressed to according to Romans 1:7?_____

_____

_____

Some scholars refer to the Book of Romans as a mini-version of the Bible or Christianity in a nutshell. One of the primary themes of Romans is justification by faith. What does Romans 3:24 say? _____

_____

_____

First and Second Corinthians: The Bible contains two letters that Paul wrote to believers in the church in Corinth. Corinth was a leading commercial center of Greece and a city known for paganism and immorality. In the first letter to the Corinthians, Paul addresses several issues of sin in the church and writes a letter of correction. In his second letter Paul defends his calling as an apostle of Christ. Why did Paul write Second Corinthians according to 2 Corinthians 13:10? _____

_____

_____

_____

Galatians: The Book of Galatians was written to churches in the Roman province called Galatia. It was written as a warning against false teaching from a group of people called Judaizers. These Jewish Christians were teaching that certain Jewish traditions must still be followed. How is this expressed in Galatians 1:6-7? _____

_____

_____

_____

Paul writes to the Galatians to show them their freedom in Christ.

Ephesians: Ephesians was a letter written to believers in the Church in Ephesus. Paul writes this letter to help believers in Ephesus understand the riches they have in Christ. How does Paul refer to these believers in Ephesians 1:1?_____

_____

_____

☐ **THURSDAY**
Ephesians
2:1-10

Philippians: Paul writes the letter to the Church in Philippi while he was under house arrest in Rome. Being a prisoner himself, Paul writes to the Philippians about rejoicing in all circumstances. What does Paul write in Philippians 3:1? _____

_____

_____

Colossians: The Book of Colossians was written to believers in a city called Colossae. The church in Colossae was dealing with a heresy that combined Jewish legalism with Gnosticism. Gnosticism taught that there was a higher truth that only the enlightened would receive. They also denied the humanity of Jesus. What other church would benefit from this letter according to Colossians 4:16?_____

_____

_____

☐ **FRIDAY**
2 Timothy
4:1-22

Thessalonians: Paul wrote the Books of First and Second Thessalonians to the church that was located in the city of Thessalonica. In the face of persecution, Paul writes First Thessalonians to encourage the church to prepare for Christ's return. In Second Thessalonians Paul writes to correct some misunderstandings from his first letter. How was the church in Thessalonica describe in 2 Thessalonians 1:3?_____

_____

_____

First and Second Timothy: Timothy was a disciple of Paul who later became a pastor in the church at Ephesus. Paul writes First Timothy to encourage him as he attempted to feed and lead the congregation in Ephesus. Why did Paul write this first letter to Timothy according to First Timothy 3:14-15? _____

_____

_____

Paul writes his final letter, 2 Timothy, from a prison cell in Rome. In this letter he encourages Timothy to fight the good fight and guard the gospel against false teaching. How did Paul see his life in 2 Timothy 4:7? ___

_____

_____

Titus: Titus is another letter to a young minister that Paul was mentoring. Titus was the pastor of the churches in Crete, and Paul writes to encourage him to appoint godly leadership, teach sound doctrine, and model a godly lifestyle. What were some of the qualifications of church leaders according to Titus 1:5-10?_____

_____

_____

_____

Philemon: Philemon is a church leader that Paul writes concerning one of his runaway slaves named Onesimus. Paul met Onesimus in prison and led him to faith in Christ. What does Paul call himself in Philemon verse 10? Paul writes to Philemon encouraging him to forgive and accept Onesimus back as a brother rather than a slave. What does Philemon verses 15 and 16 say?_

_____

PAUL'S MISSION TRIPS

Many of the letters Paul wrote were written to

churches he had started on his three missionary journeys recorded in the Book of Acts. Paul's first missionary journey is recorded in Acts 13:2 through 14:28. Where did his first journey begin? (Acts 13:1) _____

_____

Paul's second mission trip is recorded in Acts 15:36 through 18:21. What are some places Paul traveled to during this time?_____

_____

_____

Who traveled with Paul on this second mission trip? (Acts 15:40 / 16:3)_____

From Acts 18:22 to Acts 21:16 we have the account of Paul's third mission trip. What was the goal of this trip based on Acts 18:23? _____

_____

Studying Paul's three mission trips will help you connect to the epistles he wrote.

Answers to quiz: Antioch, Prison, Peter, Epaphroditus, Crete, Onesimus

QUESTIONS FOR GROUP DISCUSSION OR PERSONAL REFLECTION

➤ Open your group with prayer and share a victory you have had or a challenge you are facing.

➤ Which of Paul's letters is considered your favorite and why?

➤ Read Acts 13:2 and Acts 1:8. How do these verses connect? How do they connect with Romans 15:19? What does this mean to us today?

➤ Read 2 Corinthians 4:7-18. Describe Paul's ministry. How can this same passage encourage people today?

➤ Read Acts 26:4-11. How would you describe Paul before coming to faith in Christ? What happened after Paul encountered Christ in Acts 26:15-18? Does this still happen to people today?

➤ What does Romans 5:8 tell us about God? What does 2 Corinthians 5:20 say about us? How are you doing as an ambassador of Christ?

➤ Read 1 Timothy 4:11-16. Why do you think Paul wrote to younger pastors like Timothy? Who is the Paul in your life today?

➤ Read 2 Timothy 4:6-8. How does Paul see his life as he nears the end? How does your life compare to what Paul wrote at this point in time?

➤ What can you do to change how your story will end?

➤ Take some time to share prayer requests and pray for each other.

WEEK EIGHT: THE BOOKS OF GENERAL LETTERS AND REVELATION

Goal: To understand the General Epistles and Revelation

The last nine books of the Bible are called the "General Epistles" and the "Book of Revelation." The General Epistles were written by a number of different authors, and Revelation was a vision given to John by Jesus of the things to come. What did Jesus say to John in Revelation 1:19? _____

_____

_____

The General Epistles are comprised of several different authors, cover a wide range of subjects, and connect to an audience that was very spread out. Who were the known authors of the General Letters?_____

_____

_____

The author of Hebrews is unknown. Many believe Paul wrote it but no one knows for certain. Who were these books written to according to James 1:1? _____

According to 1 Peter 1:1? _____

The topics covered in the General Epistles range from false teaching to suffering. Each book has a different focus but combined they all help believers know how to live in a world filled with persecution while anticipating Christ's return.

Take a minute and see how much you know about the General Epistles and Revelation by answering the following questions.

WEEKLY BIBLE READING

Read the passage and write out an insight on at least one of the following:

A: Attitude to change
C: Command to obey
T: Truth to believe
S: Sin to confess

☐ **MONDAY**
Hebrews 11:1-39

What did James and Jude have in common? _____

What did Peter and John have in common? _____

Who was Second John written to? _____

Who was Third John written to? _____

Where was John while writing Revelation? _____

A QUICK LOOK

Entire books could be written about the General Epistles, but let's take a quick look at these eight very powerful books.

Hebrews: The Book of Hebrews was written to Jewish Christians to encourage them not to slip back into Judaism and abandon their faith in Christ. What does Hebrews 2:1 say? _____
_____
_____

The author of Hebrews is unknown, but the purpose is clear.

James: Most Bible scholars agree that James, the half brother of Jesus, wrote the Book of James. It was most likely written to an audience of Jewish Christians. One of the themes of the book is faith in action. What does James 2:18 say?_____
_____
_____

First Peter: Peter was an Apostle of Jesus and the author of the books First and Second Peter. These two books were written to Christians scattered throughout Asia Minor. First Peter was written to encourage believers who were facing persecution for their faith. What does 1 Peter 1:6-7 say?_____
_____
_____
_____

Second Peter: Peter wrote his second letter to deal with problems from inside the church. What was taking place according to 2 Peter 2:1? _____

_____

_____

How does 1 Peter 1:16 align with Peter being an Apostle of Jesus? _____

_____

_____

☐ **THURSDAY**
1 John 4:1-21

First John: The Book of First John is often referred to as the "Love Letter" of the Bible. The Apostle John writes of God's love for us and the need for us to love others. What does 1 John 4:7 say? _____

_____

_____

Second John: Second John is only thirteen verses long and was written to the "Elect lady and her children." Mostly likely this phrase is a reference to the Church, and John writes this letter to warn against false teaching. What does 2 John 9 teach? _____

_____

_____

☐ **FRIDAY**
Revelation
22:1-21

Third John: John's third letter is a "thank you" note to a man named Gaius. John commends Gaius for his hospitality toward traveling teachers that have stayed with him. What does 3 John 5 say? _____

_____

_____

Jude: Jude, like James, is also a half brother of Jesus. Jude writes his letter to warn against false teachers and encourages believers to remain faithful. Why does Jude write according to verse 3? _____

_____

_____

47

THINGS TO COME

PRAYER REQUESTS

_____

_____

_____

_____

_____

_____

_____

_____

_____

_____

_____

_____

_____

_____

_____

_____

_____

_____

_____

_____

_____

John wrote the Book of Revelation while a prisoner on the Island of Patmos. The purpose for this letter is given in Revelation 1:1. What does this verse say? _____

_____

_____

The word "revelation" means to disclose or unveil. This book is the unveiling of God's plan for the future. The book was given to John in a vision, and much of the book is written in symbolic fashion. The Book of Revelation can be better understood in three primary sections.

Seven Churches! The first three chapters of Revelation are messages to seven different churches in Asia Minor. In these messages God confronts what He sees taking place within His church. In some cases He commends, and in other cases He condemns. Here is one example of each. What does Revelation 3:8 say about the church in Philadelphia? _____

_____

_____

What does Revelation 3:15 say about the church in Laodicea? _____

_____

_____

Seven Symbols! In Revelation John writes of future apocalyptic events using symbols. The words John uses are seven seals, seven trumpets, and seven bowls. The seals are judgments of war, famine, persecution, poverty, and pestilence. The trumpets are judgments associated with demonic activity and include such things as part of the earth being burned and parts of the sea turning to blood. The bowl judgments take place right before Christ returns and involve such things as bodily sores, rivers turning to blood, the sun scorching the earth, and darkness covering the earth. All of these judgments illustrate how bad things will be on the earth prior to Christ's return.

Seven Events! The Book of Revelation includes seven major events that will take place at the end of time. Here is a list of these seven events and the reference in Revelation. Take time to read each reference.

The Antichrist — Revelation 13:1-10

The Mark of the Beast — Revelation 13:18

The Second Coming of Christ — Revelation 19:11-19

The Millennial Reign — Revelation 20:1-3

The Great and Final Judgment — Revelation 20:11-15

The Lake of Fire — Revelation 20:10

The New Heaven and Earth — Revelation 21:1-4

What does the Bible say about those who read the Book of Revelation? _____

_____

_____

Answers to quiz: Half brothers of Jesus, Apostles, The Elect (or Chosen) lady, Gaius, Island of Patmos

QUESTIONS FOR GROUP DISCUSSION OR PERSONAL REFLECTION

➤ Open your group with prayer and share a highlight from your week.

➤ Which of these General Letters are you most familiar with and which are you the least familiar with? Do you have a favorite?

➤ Read Hebrews 4:12 and explain how the Word of God can be a two-edged sword? How sharp is your sword these days?

➤ Read James 3:5-12 and describe the problems the tongue can cause? Have you ever seen this happen? How do we keep from allowing this to happen?

➤ Read 1 Peter 2:9-12. What does this passage say about the way we should live? How well are your actions glorifying the Father these days? Where could you improve?

➤ Read 1 John 2:15-17. How should we view the world we live in? How do we resist the lure of the world?

➤ Read Jude 17-21. What must we be on guard against? What is the best way to keep from having false teachers attack the church?

➤ Read Revelation 7:9-12. What do you think heaven will be like? What should we do between now and the time Christ returns?

➤ Take some time to share prayer requests and pray for each other.

A FEW FINAL THOUGHTS...

Congratulations! You have finished *Bible Essentials*. Hopefully, you have applied yourself wholeheartedly to this study and are growing as a disciple of Christ.

Now you know some of the essential truths of the Scriptures. If you continue to read, study, and apply the truth of The Bible you will grow closer to God and become more like Christ.

It is time now to take your next step as a disciple and work through another course in the Disciple Making Essentials Series. You may also want to check out more resources from Impact Ministries. Check out the Impact Ministries page in the back of this booklet or look us up on the web at impactdisciples.com.

KEEP READING THE WORD!

 IMPACT

Inspiring People and Churches to Be and Build Disciples of Jesus Christ

EXPLORE

We invite you to EXPLORE and DISCOVER the concepts of DISCIPLE MAKING by checking out the following RESOURCES.

◆The Impact Blog ◆The Impact Newsletter
◆The Impact Audio and Video Podcasts

EDUCATE

We encourage you to LEARN more about DISCIPLE MAKING through our written RESOURCES and TRAINING opportunities.

◆The DMC Training ◆315 Leadership Training ◆Free Resources

ESTABLISH

We seek to HELP you start a DISCIPLE MAKING MOVEMENT by showing you how to LAUNCH a disciple making group.

◆The Impact Weekend ◆The Essentials ◆Vision Consultation

ENGAGE

We invite you to JOIN with Impact Ministries in spreading the VISION of DISCIPLE MAKING around the WORLD through several involvement opportunities.

◆Join our Prayer Team ◆Be an Impact Trainer ◆Partner with Us

CONTACT US

◆ImpactDisciples.com ◆Info@ImpactDisciples.com ◆678.854.9322

Made in the USA
Middletown, DE
17 May 2020